Safe Haven

A Parent's Guide

to School Safety

&

Gun Violence

Prevention

Lillian Prescott

EDU Publishing

Foreword

As the author of "Safe Haven: A Parent's Guide to School Safety and Gun Violence Prevention," I am deeply committed to helping parents and children navigate the complex and challenging subject of school safety in today's world.

Our children deserve to grow up in a world where they can learn and thrive without fear. Unfortunately, school safety and gun violence have become pressing issues that cannot be ignored. This realization prompted me to delve into research, consulting with experts in various fields, and gathering firsthand accounts from parents, educators, and students affected by these issues.

In writing this book, my primary goal has been to provide parents with a comprehensive resource that not only raises awareness about the realities of school safety and gun violence but also offers practical guidance on how to address and prevent these issues in their children's lives. From understanding the warning signs of potential threats to learning effective communication strategies, this guide aims to empower parents with the information they need to make informed decisions and take proactive steps to protect their children.

Throughout the pages of "Safe Haven," you will find a wealth of information, advice, and resources designed to help you and your family navigate the complexities of this difficult subject. My hope is that by sharing this knowledge, we can work together to create a safer and more secure future for our children.

As you read this book, I encourage you to keep an open mind and to engage in conversations with your family, friends, and community members. It is through open dialogue and collective action that we can truly make a difference in the lives of our children.

Thank you for joining me on this journey. It is my sincere hope that "Safe Haven: A Parent's Guide to School Safety and Gun Violence Prevention" serves as a valuable resource, providing guidance, support, and inspiration as we work together to create a safer world for our children.

With warm regards,

Professor Lillian Prescott

Overview

"Safe Steps: A Parent's Guide to Preparing Young Children for School Safety and Navigating Gun Violence" is an essential resource for parents with children in the United States. As gun violence continues to pose a significant threat to the safety and well-being of students, it is crucial for parents to educate and prepare their children to face and address such situations. This book provides practical guidance and strategies to help parents navigate these difficult conversations and develop a safety plan tailored to their child's needs.

The book is divided into three sections, each consisting of six chapters.

Section 1: Building a Foundation of Safety
This section explores the importance of creating a safe and nurturing home environment where children feel comfortable discussing their fears and concerns. It provides tips for parents on how to foster open communication, develop their child's emotional intelligence, and instill a sense of security and confidence.

Section 2: Talking About School Safety and Gun Violence
This section delves into the difficult conversations surrounding school safety and gun violence. It provides age-appropriate guidance on how to discuss these topics with children, as well as advice on addressing their questions and concerns. This section also includes suggestions for teaching children about warning signs and reporting suspicious behavior, as well as the importance of lockdown drills and other safety procedures.

Section 3: Preparing for Emergencies
In this section, parents will learn how to create a comprehensive safety plan for their child, including establishing a safe meeting place and creating an emergency contact list. Additionally, it covers how to help children cope with the emotional aftermath of a school shooting or other traumatic events, as well as resources for mental health support and counseling services.

"Safe Steps: A Parent's Guide to Preparing Young Children for School Safety and Navigating Gun Violence" empowers parents to take an active role in their child's safety and well-being at school. With practical advice, age-appropriate strategies, and a compassionate approach, this book is a valuable tool for parents seeking to prepare their children for the challenges of today's world.

Table Of Contents

Section 3: Preparing for Emergencies

Section 1: Building a Foundation of Safety

Chapter 1: Setting the Stage for Open Communication

Chapter 2: Emotional Intelligence and Empathy

Chapter 3: Building Trust and Confidence

Chapter 4: Creating a Safe and Supportive Home Environment

Chapter 5: Navigating Difficult Conversations with Your Child

Chapter 6: Encouraging Resilience and Adaptability

Chapter 1: Setting the Stage for Open Communication

Introduction

Effective communication is the cornerstone of a strong parent-child relationship. Establishing open and honest communication with your child is essential for building trust, creating a safe space for them to express their thoughts and feelings, and helping them navigate the challenges they may face in school, including gun violence and safety concerns. In this chapter, we will explore practical tips for fostering open communication, creating a judgment-free environment, and using active listening and effective communication techniques.

Creating a Judgment-Free Environment

Children are more likely to share their thoughts, fears, and concerns if they feel their parents will not judge, criticize, or dismiss them. To create a judgment-free environment:

Show empathy: Validate your child's feelings by acknowledging and empathizing with their emotions, whether it's fear, confusion, or anxiety.

Be patient: Allow your child to express themselves without interrupting or finishing their sentences. Give them the time they need to find the right words and articulate their feelings.

Encourage honesty: Make it clear to your child that you value their honesty, even if it's something that may be difficult for you to hear. Assure them that you will always be there to listen and support them.

Remain calm and composed: If your child shares something that concerns or upsets you, try to remain calm and composed. Your reaction will influence their willingness to share in the future.

Active Listening and Effective Communication Techniques

Active listening is essential for truly understanding your child's feelings and concerns. It involves focusing your attention on the speaker, providing feedback, and demonstrating understanding. To practice active listening:

Make eye contact: Establishing eye contact with your child while they're speaking shows that you're engaged and attentive.

Use verbal and non-verbal cues: Nodding, smiling, or using phrases like "I see" or "I understand" can help your child feel heard and understood.

Reflect and clarify: To ensure you understand your child's message, reflect on their words by paraphrasing or summarizing what they've said. Ask clarifying questions if you need more information.

Avoid distractions: Put away your phone or any other distractions when engaging in conversations with your child, showing that you're fully present and attentive.

Be open-minded: Approach conversations with an open mind and resist the urge to jump to conclusions or make assumptions.

Conclusion

Open and honest communication is key to helping your child feel safe discussing school safety and gun violence. By creating a judgment-free environment and practicing active listening, you'll foster a strong relationship with your child, making it easier for them to share their thoughts and concerns. In the following chapters, we'll discuss strategies for building emotional intelligence, trust, and a secure home environment that supports open communication and prepares your child to face the challenges of today's world.

Chapter 2: Emotional Intelligence and Empathy

Introduction

Emotional intelligence and empathy are essential components of your child's development, as they contribute to their overall well-being, resilience, and ability to form healthy relationships. By teaching your child to identify, understand, and manage their emotions, and fostering empathy and compassion towards others, you are equipping them with invaluable skills that will serve them throughout their lives. In this chapter, we will explore the importance of emotional intelligence and empathy, as well as strategies for nurturing these essential skills in your child.

The Importance of Emotional Intelligence

Emotional intelligence refers to the ability to identify, understand, and manage one's own emotions, as well as the emotions of others. Children with high emotional intelligence tend to have better relationships with their peers, are more resilient in the face of adversity, and are better able to cope with the challenges they encounter in school and beyond. Some key components of emotional intelligence include:

   Self-awareness: The ability to recognize and understand one's own emotions.
   Self-regulation: The ability to manage one's emotions in a healthy and appropriate manner.
   Social awareness: The ability to recognize and understand the emotions of others.
   Relationship management: The ability to establish and maintain healthy relationships with others.

Nurturing Emotional Intelligence in Your Child

To help your child develop emotional intelligence, consider the following strategies:

Encourage emotional expression: Provide opportunities for your child to express their emotions through conversation, art, writing, or other creative outlets. Validate their emotions and encourage them to talk about their feelings.

Teach emotion vocabulary: Help your child develop a rich emotional vocabulary by teaching them words to describe their feelings. Encourage them to use these words when discussing their emotions.

Model emotional intelligence: Demonstrate emotional intelligence in your own actions and behavior. Show your child how you identify, understand, and manage your emotions in various situations.

Encourage problem-solving: Teach your child to approach emotional challenges with a problem-solving mindset, helping them develop strategies for managing their emotions effectively.

Fostering Empathy and Compassion

Empathy is the ability to understand and share the feelings of others, while compassion involves responding to the suffering of others with care and a desire to help. To foster empathy and compassion in your child, consider the following techniques:

Model empathetic behavior: Show empathy towards others in your daily interactions, demonstrating to your child how to be compassionate and understanding.

Encourage perspective-taking: Help your child understand and appreciate the feelings and perspectives of others by asking them to imagine how they might feel in a similar situation.

Provide opportunities for helping others: Involve your child in community service, volunteering, or other activities that allow them to help others and develop a sense of empathy and compassion.

Discuss empathy in stories and media: Use books, movies, and other media as opportunities to discuss empathy, compassion, and the importance of understanding others' feelings.

Conclusion

By nurturing emotional intelligence and empathy in your child, you are not only promoting their personal growth but also preparing them to navigate the challenges of school safety and gun violence with resilience and understanding. In the next chapters, we will explore additional strategies for building a strong foundation of safety, including establishing trust and confidence, creating a safe and supportive home environment, and navigating difficult conversations with your child.

Chapter 3: Building Trust and Confidence

Introduction

Establishing trust and confidence is vital for your child's well-being, self-esteem, and resilience in the face of adversity. When children trust their parents and have confidence in their own abilities, they are better equipped to handle challenging situations, including school safety concerns and gun violence. In this chapter, we will discuss strategies for building trust and confidence, fostering a strong parent-child relationship, and promoting self-reliance and problem-solving skills in your child.

Building Trust with Your Child

Trust is the foundation of a strong parent-child relationship. To build trust with your child:

Be consistent: Consistency in your actions and responses helps your child feel secure, knowing what to expect from you.

Keep your promises: When you make promises to your child, do your best to follow through on them. If circumstances change and you're unable to keep a promise, explain the situation and apologize.

Be honest: Always be truthful with your child, even when discussing difficult topics. This encourages your child to be honest with you in return.

Show respect: Treat your child with respect and listen to their opinions and feelings, even if you don't always agree with them.

Provide emotional support: Be there for your child during both good times and bad, offering a listening ear, comfort, and guidance when needed.

Fostering Confidence in Your Child

Confidence plays a crucial role in helping your child face challenges and feel secure in their abilities. To foster confidence in your child:

Encourage independence: Allow your child to make age-appropriate choices and take on responsibilities, giving them the opportunity to learn and grow from their experiences.

Praise effort, not just results: Recognize and acknowledge your child's efforts, even if they don't always achieve the desired outcome. This helps them understand the value of perseverance and hard work.

Help them set realistic goals: Work with your child to set achievable goals and break them down into manageable steps. Celebrate their accomplishments along the way.

Foster problem-solving skills: Encourage your child to approach challenges with a problem-solving mindset, guiding them through the process of identifying potential solutions and evaluating their effectiveness.

Be a positive role model: Demonstrate confidence in your own abilities and model a healthy attitude toward failure and setbacks, showing your child that it's okay to make mistakes and learn from them.

Conclusion

Building trust and confidence in your child is essential for helping
them feel secure and capable of navigating the challenges they may
encounter, including school safety and gun violence. As you work
to strengthen your parent-child relationship and promote self-
reliance and problem-solving skills, you are laying the groundwork
for a solid foundation of safety. In the following chapters, we will
explore additional strategies for creating a secure and supportive
home environment, navigating difficult conversations, and
preparing your child for the realities of school safety.

Chapter 4: Creating a Safe and Supportive Home Environment

Introduction

A safe and supportive home environment is crucial for your child's well-being, as it provides a foundation of stability and security that helps them navigate the challenges they may face, including school safety and gun violence. In this chapter, we will discuss strategies for creating a home environment that promotes safety, well-being, and a sense of security, including designing a child-friendly space, establishing routines, and setting boundaries and expectations.

Designing a Child-Friendly Space

To create a home environment that fosters a sense of safety and security:

Make your home physically safe: Ensure your home is free from hazards that could harm your child, such as sharp edges, unsecured furniture, and dangerous chemicals. Install safety devices like smoke alarms, carbon monoxide detectors, and fire extinguishers.

Create a comfortable atmosphere: Design a space that is warm, inviting, and calming, with plenty of natural light, soft textures, and soothing colors.

Provide a designated space for your child: Offer a dedicated area for your child to relax, play, and express themselves, such as a bedroom, playroom, or reading nook.

Encourage organization: Help your child keep their belongings organized and easily accessible, teaching them responsibility and reinforcing a sense of order and control.

Establishing Routines

Routines provide structure and predictability, which can be comforting to children and help them feel secure. To establish routines:

Develop consistent daily routines: Create routines for waking up, bedtime, mealtimes, and other daily activities, helping your child understand what to expect throughout the day.

Involve your child in creating routines: Include your child in the process of establishing routines, allowing them to have input and take ownership of their daily schedule.

Be flexible: While routines are important, remember to be flexible and adapt as needed, accommodating changes in your child's needs or schedule.

Setting Boundaries and Expectations

Clear boundaries and expectations can help your child feel secure and understand the limits of acceptable behavior. To set boundaries and expectations:

Establish clear rules: Set clear and age-appropriate rules for behavior, explaining the reasons behind the rules and the consequences for breaking them.

Be consistent with consequences: Apply consequences consistently when rules are broken, helping your child understand the cause and effect of their actions.

Encourage open communication: Foster a climate of open communication, allowing your child to express their feelings and opinions about the rules and boundaries.

Balance autonomy with guidance: Encourage your child to make choices and decisions within the established boundaries, while providing guidance and support when needed.

Conclusion

Creating a safe and supportive home environment is essential for helping your child feel secure and capable of navigating the challenges they may face, including school safety and gun violence. By designing a child-friendly space, establishing routines, and setting boundaries and expectations, you are reinforcing a sense of safety and stability that will serve as a found

Chapter 5: Navigating Difficult Conversations with Your Child

Introduction

Discussing difficult topics, such as school safety and gun violence, can be challenging for parents. It is essential to approach these conversations in an age-appropriate manner, maintaining open dialogue as your child grows and their understanding of the world evolves. In this chapter, we will provide guidance on how to navigate difficult conversations with your child, ensuring they feel informed, supported, and safe.

Age-Appropriate Conversations

To ensure your conversations are appropriate for your child's age and understanding:

Know your child's developmental stage: Familiarize yourself with your child's cognitive and emotional development, tailoring your conversations to their level of understanding.

Use simple and clear language: Communicate using straightforward language that your child can comprehend, avoiding overly technical or abstract terms.

Limit exposure to graphic details: Be cautious about sharing graphic or disturbing details that may be too overwhelming for your child to process.

Encourage questions: Invite your child to ask questions and express their concerns, providing honest and age-appropriate answers.

Revisit the topic as needed: As your child grows and their understanding evolves, continue to discuss difficult topics, updating the information and addressing any new concerns that may arise.

Strategies for Navigating Difficult Conversations

To navigate difficult conversations effectively:

Choose the right time and place: Select a quiet and comfortable setting where your child feels relaxed and can focus on the conversation without distractions.

Be calm and reassuring: Approach the conversation with a calm demeanor, reassuring your child that you are there to support and protect them.

Listen actively: Pay close attention to your child's words, emotions, and body language, responding with empathy and understanding.

Validate their feelings: Acknowledge and validate your child's emotions, letting them know that it is normal to feel scared or worried about difficult topics.

Offer practical solutions: Provide your child with concrete steps they can take to feel safer, such as following school safety procedures, reporting suspicious behavior, or practicing emergency drills.

Maintaining Open Dialogue

To keep the lines of communication open:

Establish a routine for check-ins: Schedule regular check-ins with your child to discuss their feelings, concerns, and any new developments related to difficult topics.

Foster a judgment-free environment: Encourage open communication by creating a judgment-free environment where your child feels comfortable expressing their thoughts and emotions.

Be patient: Understand that your child may need time to process difficult topics and may not be ready to discuss them immediately.

Keep yourself informed: Stay up-to-date on current events and issues related to school safety and gun violence, ensuring you are prepared to answer your child's questions and address their concerns.

Conclusion

Navigating difficult conversations with your child is an essential aspect of building a foundation of safety. By approaching these discussions in an age-appropriate manner and maintaining open dialogue, you can help your child feel informed, supported, and secure. In the following sections, we will delve deeper into specific topics related to school safety and gun violence, providing guidance on how to discuss these issues with your child and prepare them for the challenges they may face.

Chapter 6: Encouraging Resilience and Adaptability

Introduction

Fostering resilience and adaptability in children is crucial for helping them navigate the challenges they may face, including issues related to school safety and gun violence. Resilient and adaptable children are better equipped to cope with challenges, overcome obstacles, and develop a growth mindset that will serve them well in the face of adversity. In this chapter, we will explore strategies for teaching children resilience and adaptability, laying the groundwork for a strong foundation of safety.

Understanding Resilience and Adaptability

Resilience is the ability to recover from setbacks and adapt to change, while adaptability is the capacity to adjust to new situations and environments. Together, these qualities help children:

Cope with stress and challenges: Resilient and adaptable children are better equipped to handle stress and overcome challenges, both in school and in life.

Learn from failure: By developing a growth mindset, children learn to view failure as an opportunity to grow and improve, rather than as a permanent setback.

Build problem-solving skills: Resilience and adaptability enable children to approach problems with creativity and resourcefulness, seeking solutions rather than dwelling on obstacles.

Strategies for Encouraging Resilience and Adaptability

To help your child develop resilience and adaptability:

Model resilient behavior: Demonstrate resilience and adaptability in your own life, showing your child how to bounce back from setbacks and adapt to change.

Provide opportunities for problem-solving: Encourage your child to take on challenges and solve problems, offering guidance and support when needed but allowing them to work through difficulties independently.

Teach coping strategies: Equip your child with coping strategies, such as deep breathing, mindfulness, or self-talk, to help them manage stress and negative emotions.

Encourage a growth mindset: Praise effort and persistence, rather than focusing on outcomes or innate abilities, to help your child develop a growth mindset that values learning and improvement.

Foster strong relationships: Encourage your child to build and maintain strong relationships with family, friends, and mentors, providing a support network that can bolster their resilience and adaptability.

Provide opportunities for reflection: Encourage your child to reflect on their experiences, both positive and negative, to help them identify areas for growth and improvement.

Celebrate small victories: Acknowledge and celebrate your child's achievements and progress, no matter how small, to reinforce their sense of accomplishment and boost their confidence.

Conclusion

Encouraging resilience and adaptability in your child is a vital component of building a foundation of safety. By teaching them how to cope with challenges, overcome obstacles, and develop a growth mindset, you are preparing them to face adversity with confidence and determination. As we move into the next sections of this book, we will explore strategies for discussing school safety and gun violence with your child, as well as preparing them for emergencies and other difficult situations.

Section 2: Talking About School Safety and Gun Violence

Chapter 1: Age-Appropriate Conversations on School Safety and Gun Violence

Introduction

Discussing school safety and gun violence with children can be a daunting task for parents. It is crucial to tailor these conversations to the child's age, developmental stage, and emotional maturity to ensure they feel informed, supported, and safe. In this chapter, we will provide guidelines on how to approach these conversations in an age-appropriate manner.

Preschoolers (Ages 3-5)

At this age, children are still developing their understanding of the world and may struggle to comprehend complex topics like gun violence. Focus on:

Reassurance: Emphasize that you and their teachers are there to keep them safe and that the adults in their life are working to protect them.

Basic safety rules: Teach them simple safety rules, such as staying with their teacher and following instructions during drills or emergencies.

Listening to their feelings: Encourage your child to express their emotions and concerns, offering comfort and validation.

Elementary School (Ages 6-10)

As children enter elementary school, they become more aware of the world around them and may have heard about school shootings or gun violence. Focus on:

Age-appropriate explanations: Provide simple, honest explanations about school safety and gun violence, avoiding graphic details or overly technical language.

Safety procedures: Discuss the importance of lockdown drills, fire drills, and other safety procedures in school, reassuring them that these measures are in place to keep them safe.

Reporting concerns: Encourage your child to share any concerns or suspicions with a trusted adult, emphasizing the importance of speaking up to protect themselves and others.

Middle School (Ages 11-13)

By middle school, children have a more mature understanding of the world and may have strong opinions about gun violence and school safety. Focus on:

Open dialogue: Engage in open, honest conversations about school safety and gun violence, answering their questions and addressing their concerns.

Building critical thinking skills: Encourage your child to think critically about the issues surrounding gun violence and school safety, discussing potential solutions and the importance of advocacy.

Emotional support: Recognize that discussions about gun violence can be emotionally charged, and be prepared to offer support and validation for your child's feelings.

Conclusion

Approaching conversations about school safety and gun violence in an age-appropriate manner is essential for ensuring that your child feels informed, supported, and secure. By adapting your language and focus based on your child's age and developmental stage, you can help them understand these complex issues while maintaining their sense of safety and well-being. In the following chapters, we will delve deeper into specific topics related to school safety and gun violence, providing further guidance on how to discuss these issues with your children.

Chapter 2: Addressing Questions and Concerns

Introduction

Children may have various questions and concerns about school safety and gun violence as they become more aware of these issues. It is essential to address their inquiries with honesty and sensitivity, providing age-appropriate information and reassurance. In this chapter, we will guide you through handling your child's questions and concerns in a supportive and empathetic manner.

Listen and Validate

When your child approaches you with a question or concern, begin by actively listening and validating their feelings. Acknowledge their emotions, let them know that it's okay to feel scared or worried, and reassure them that their feelings are normal.

Provide Age-Appropriate Information

When answering your child's questions, tailor your response to their age and developmental stage. Offer clear, honest explanations without overwhelming them with complex or graphic details. It's important to strike a balance between providing accurate information and preserving their sense of safety.

Offer Reassurance

Reassure your child that many people, including parents, teachers, and law enforcement, are working to ensure their safety at school. Remind them of the safety procedures in place, such as lockdown drills and emergency plans, and emphasize that these measures help keep them safe.

Encourage Open Dialogue

Let your child know that they can always come to you with their questions and concerns, and maintain open lines of communication. Regularly check in with them about their feelings and any new questions that may arise, ensuring they feel supported and heard.

Be Honest About Uncertainty

In some cases, you may not have all the answers to your child's questions. It's okay to admit that you don't know everything and use it as an opportunity to research and learn together. This approach models humility and demonstrates the value of seeking information.

Connect with Resources

If your child's questions or concerns extend beyond your expertise, consider connecting them with appropriate resources. This might include school counselors, mental health professionals, or community organizations that can provide additional support and information.

Conclusion

Addressing your child's questions and concerns about school safety and gun violence is a crucial aspect of supporting their emotional well-being. By actively listening, providing age-appropriate information, and offering reassurance, you can help your child navigate these difficult topics with confidence. In the next chapter, we will explore the importance of teaching children about warning signs and reporting suspicious behavior to further enhance their safety and preparedness.

Chapter 3: Teaching Children About Warning Signs and Reporting Suspicious Behavior

Introduction

Equipping children with the knowledge to identify warning signs and report suspicious behavior is a vital component of promoting school safety. In this chapter, we will discuss how to teach your child about potential warning signs of violence and the importance of sharing their concerns with a trusted adult.

Identifying Warning Signs

Teach your child that certain behaviors and situations may indicate a potential threat. Some warning signs to look for include:

Excessive interest in weapons or acts of violence
Severe mood swings or sudden changes in behavior
Social isolation or withdrawal from friends and activities
Threats or hints of violence, either in person or online
Unusual or alarming statements or writings

Remind your child that these signs do not automatically mean someone will engage in violence, but they should still be taken seriously and reported.

Reporting Suspicious Behavior

Encourage your child to share any concerns or observations with a trusted adult, such as a parent, teacher, or school counselor. Emphasize that they should not try to handle the situation alone and that reporting is a crucial step in keeping themselves and others safe. Discuss the following reporting tips with your child:

Be specific: When reporting suspicious behavior, encourage your child to provide as much detail as possible, including the person's name, what they observed, and when and where the incident occurred.

Stay calm: Remind your child to remain calm and composed when reporting their concerns. This approach will help ensure that they are taken seriously and that the information is conveyed accurately.

Maintain confidentiality: Assure your child that their identity will be kept confidential when reporting concerns, and that they will not be labeled as a "tattletale" or "snitch" for doing so.

Role-Playing and Practice

To help your child become more comfortable with reporting suspicious behavior, consider role-playing different scenarios. This exercise will provide them with an opportunity to practice communicating their concerns effectively and allow you to offer guidance and feedback.

Reinforcing the Importance of Reporting

Regularly remind your child of the importance of reporting suspicious behavior and warning signs, emphasizing that their actions could help prevent a dangerous situation. Encourage open dialogue and keep communication lines open, so your child feels comfortable discussing their concerns with you.

Conclusion

Teaching children about warning signs and the importance of reporting suspicious behavior is a vital step in promoting school safety and preventing potential acts of violence. By providing your child with the necessary tools and fostering open communication, you can empower them to contribute to a safer and more secure learning environment. In the following chapters, we will continue to explore strategies for discussing school safety and gun violence, including the significance of lockdown drills and other safety procedures.

Chapter 4: The Role of Lockdown Drills and Safety Procedures

Introduction

Lockdown drills and safety procedures play a crucial role in preparing schools and students for potential emergency situations. As a parent, it's important to understand their significance and help your child comprehend their purpose without causing undue fear or anxiety. In this chapter, we will explore how to discuss lockdown drills with your child and emphasize the importance of adhering to safety protocols.

Explaining Lockdown Drills and Safety Procedures

Begin by explaining to your child that lockdown drills are practiced to ensure everyone knows what to do in case of an emergency, just like fire drills. Emphasize that the goal is to keep everyone safe, and practicing these drills helps students, teachers, and staff respond efficiently if an actual emergency occurs.

Using Age-Appropriate Language

When discussing lockdown drills and safety procedures, use language that is appropriate for your child's age and developmental level. Avoid using graphic or frightening details, and focus on the importance of following instructions and staying calm during drills.

Addressing Fears and Anxiety

Acknowledge that lockdown drills may be scary or unsettling for your child, and validate their feelings. Reassure them that these drills are designed to keep them safe, and that the chances of an actual emergency occurring are very low. Encourage your child to share any concerns or fears they may have, and remind them that you and their teachers are there to support and protect them.

Reinforcing the Importance of Following Safety Protocols

Stress the significance of listening to teachers and following safety procedures during lockdown drills and actual emergencies. Discuss the importance of staying quiet, following instructions, and remaining calm in such situations. Remind your child that adhering to these guidelines will help keep them and others safe.

Staying Informed About Your School's Safety Procedures

As a parent, it's important to stay informed about the safety procedures and protocols in place at your child's school. Attend parent-teacher conferences, school safety meetings, and other relevant events to stay up-to-date on the latest information and ensure you're prepared to discuss these topics with your child.

Conclusion

Understanding the role of lockdown drills and safety procedures is an essential aspect of school safety and gun violence prevention. By discussing these topics with your child in an age-appropriate and non-threatening manner, you can help alleviate their fears and ensure they are prepared to respond effectively in case of an emergency. In the next chapter, we will delve into the importance of fostering a sense of community and the role it plays in promoting school safety.

Chapter 5: Building a Support System at School

Introduction

A strong support system at school plays a vital role in ensuring your child's safety and well-being. By fostering relationships with teachers, school counselors, and other staff members, you can create a network of support for your child that promotes a safe and nurturing environment. In this chapter, we will discuss ways to collaborate with school personnel and build a strong support system for your child.

Partnering with Teachers

Developing a collaborative relationship with your child's teachers is crucial for addressing any concerns related to school safety and gun violence. Attend parent-teacher conferences and other school events to maintain open communication with teachers. Share any concerns or insights you have about your child's well-being and work together to create a safe and supportive environment in the classroom.

Engaging with School Counselors

School counselors can provide valuable resources and guidance to help children cope with anxiety, fear, and other emotions related to school safety and gun violence. Reach out to the school counselor to discuss any concerns you may have and to develop a plan for supporting your child. Encourage your child to speak with the counselor if they are experiencing difficulties or need someone to talk to about their concerns.

Connecting with Other School Staff

In addition to teachers and counselors, it's essential to establish relationships with other school staff members, such as administrators, security personnel, and support staff. These individuals can offer additional insight and assistance in creating a safe and nurturing environment for your child.

Participating in School Safety Initiatives

Many schools have safety committees or other initiatives in place to address concerns related to school safety and gun violence. Get involved in these efforts by volunteering your time, attending meetings, or providing input and feedback. Your active participation will demonstrate your commitment to ensuring a safe environment for your child and their peers.

Encouraging Peer Support

Fostering a sense of community among your child's peers can help create a supportive network that promotes safety and well-being. Encourage your child to develop friendships, engage in group activities, and participate in school clubs and organizations. A strong sense of belonging can help children feel more comfortable discussing their concerns and seeking support from their peers.

Conclusion

Building a strong support system at school is a critical aspect of addressing school safety and gun violence. By collaborating with teachers, counselors, and other staff members, you can create a safe and supportive environment for your child. In the final chapter of this section, we will explore strategies for staying informed about school safety issues and advocating for effective policies and procedures to protect all students.

Chapter 6: Empowering Children to Take Responsibility for Their Safety

Introduction

Teaching children to take responsibility for their safety is an essential aspect of addressing school safety and gun violence prevention. By empowering children with the knowledge and skills to make smart decisions, stand up against bullying, and seek help from trusted adults, you can help them develop a sense of control and agency in their well-being. In this chapter, we will explore strategies for teaching children these important skills.

Making Smart Decisions

Encourage your child to think critically and make smart decisions in various situations. Discuss the importance of assessing potential risks, considering the consequences of their actions, and making choices that prioritize their safety and well-being. Use real-life scenarios to help them practice decision-making skills and reinforce the importance of using sound judgment.

Standing Up Against Bullying

Bullying can have a significant impact on a child's sense of safety and security at school. Teach your child to recognize and stand up against bullying behavior, whether it's directed at them or someone else. Discuss the importance of treating others with respect and kindness, and encourage them to report incidents of bullying to a trusted adult.

Developing Self-Advocacy Skills

Help your child develop self-advocacy skills by teaching them how to effectively communicate their needs, concerns, and boundaries. Encourage them to express their feelings and stand up for themselves in a respectful and assertive manner. By learning to advocate for their safety and well-being, children can feel more empowered and in control of their environment.

Seeking Help from Trusted Adults

Teach your child the importance of seeking help from trusted adults when they feel unsafe or need assistance. Identify specific adults, such as teachers, school counselors, or family members, whom they can turn to for support. Encourage open communication and emphasize that it's always okay to ask for help when needed.

Practicing Safety Skills

Reinforce safety skills by regularly practicing them with your child. Discuss what to do in various emergency situations, such as lockdowns, natural disasters, or encountering a stranger. Review safety rules and protocols, and encourage your child to apply these skills in their daily lives.

Conclusion

Empowering children to take responsibility for their safety is a vital component of addressing school safety and gun violence prevention. By teaching them the skills to make smart decisions, stand up against bullying, and seek help from trusted adults, you can help your child develop a sense of control and agency in their well-being. In the next section of the book, we will explore strategies for preparing for emergencies and supporting children in the aftermath of traumatic events.

Section 3: Preparing for Emergencies

Chapter 1: Creating a Comprehensive Safety Plan

Introduction

Having a comprehensive safety plan in place is crucial for ensuring your child's well-being in the event of an emergency. This chapter will guide you through the process of developing a personalized safety plan for your child, including assessing potential risks, creating an emergency contact list, and establishing a safe meeting place for your family.

Assessing Potential Risks

The first step in creating a safety plan is to identify potential risks that your child may encounter at school or in your community. Consider factors such as the location of your child's school, its proximity to busy roads or hazardous areas, and the prevalence of crime or violence in the area. Understanding the potential risks will help you develop a tailored plan that addresses your child's specific needs.

Creating an Emergency Contact List

An essential component of your child's safety plan is a comprehensive emergency contact list. This list should include contact information for trusted family members, friends, neighbors, and other individuals who can assist your child in the event of an emergency. Ensure that your child is familiar with the list and knows how to reach these individuals if necessary.

Establishing a Safe Meeting Place

In case of an emergency that requires your child to leave school or another location, it's important to have a designated safe meeting place where your family can reunite. This location should be easily accessible, well-known to all family members, and a reasonable distance from potential hazards. Make sure your child knows the address and any landmarks that can help them find the meeting place.

Developing a Communication Plan

A clear communication plan is essential for staying connected with your child during an emergency. Establish a method for communicating with your child, whether it's through text messages, phone calls, or an alternative means of communication. Make sure your child knows how to use the chosen method and feels comfortable reaching out if they need help or reassurance.

Reviewing and Practicing the Safety Plan

Once you have developed a comprehensive safety plan, it's important to review and practice it with your child regularly. Discuss the different components of the plan, and ensure that your child understands their role and responsibilities. Conducting regular drills and revisiting the plan will help your child feel more confident and prepared in the event of an emergency.

Conclusion

Creating a comprehensive safety plan is a critical aspect of preparing for emergencies and ensuring your child's safety at school. By assessing potential risks, creating an emergency contact list, and establishing a safe meeting place, you can equip your child with the tools and knowledge they need to stay safe during challenging situations. In the following chapters, we will explore additional strategies for supporting your child during emergencies and helping them cope with the emotional aftermath of a traumatic event.

Chapter 2: Teaching Children Emergency Procedures and Drills

Introduction

Teaching children about emergency procedures and drills is an essential aspect of preparing them for potential emergencies at school. This chapter will provide guidance on how to explain and practice lockdown, evacuation, and shelter-in-place drills in an age-appropriate and empowering manner.

Lockdown Drills

Lockdown drills are designed to protect students and staff from threats within the school building. Explain to your child that during a lockdown, they will be required to remain in their classroom or another designated safe area with the door locked and lights turned off. Emphasize the importance of remaining quiet and following the teacher's instructions. To practice a lockdown drill at home, designate a safe room and have your child practice moving quickly and quietly to that room.

Evacuation Drills

Evacuation drills are used to safely exit the school building in the event of a fire or other emergency. Teach your child the importance of staying calm, listening to instructions, and following the designated evacuation route. Reinforce the need to leave personal belongings behind and to exit the building in a single-file line. At home, you can practice evacuation drills by designating an exit route and an outdoor meeting place for your family.

Shelter-in-Place Drills

Shelter-in-place drills are implemented when there is a threat outside the school building, such as severe weather or a hazardous materials incident. Explain to your child that during a shelter-in-place drill, they will be required to stay inside the school building and move to a designated safe area. Discuss the importance of following instructions and staying calm. You can practice shelter-in-place drills at home by identifying a safe area, such as a basement or interior room without windows.

Making Drills Age-Appropriate and Empowering

When discussing emergency procedures and drills with your child, it's important to use age-appropriate language and explanations. Focus on the purpose of the drills and emphasize that they are intended to keep everyone safe. Encourage your child to ask questions and express their feelings, and reassure them that it's normal to feel nervous or scared during drills. Emphasize that by practicing and following the established procedures, they are taking an active role in their own safety.

Communicating with School Staff

Stay informed about your child's school's emergency procedures and drill schedules. Communicate with teachers and administrators about any concerns or questions you may have regarding your child's understanding of and participation in drills. By staying engaged with the school, you can ensure that your child feels supported and well-prepared for potential emergencies.

Conclusion

Teaching children about emergency procedures and drills is a critical part of preparing them for school emergencies. By explaining and practicing lockdown, evacuation, and shelter-in-place drills in an age-appropriate and empowering manner, you can help your child feel confident and capable in the face of potential challenges. In the next chapter, we will discuss strategies for helping children cope with the emotional aftermath of a school shooting or other traumatic events.

Chapter 3: Building a Support Network for Emergencies

Introduction

In times of crisis, a strong support network can make all the difference in ensuring the safety and well-being of your child. This chapter will provide guidance on how to establish a support network for emergencies, including friends, family members, and neighbors. It will also cover how to create a communication plan and ensure that everyone in the network is informed and prepared to act in the event of an emergency.

Identifying Key Members of Your Support Network

Begin by identifying key individuals who can be part of your support network, such as close friends, family members, neighbors, and other parents from your child's school. These individuals should be trustworthy, reliable, and able to provide assistance during emergencies.

Establishing Roles and Responsibilities

Assign roles and responsibilities to each member of your support network based on their strengths, availability, and proximity to your child's school. For example, one person may be responsible for picking up your child from school, while another may be in charge of providing temporary shelter in case of an emergency.

Creating a Communication Plan

Develop a communication plan that outlines how you will share information and updates with your support network during an emergency. This may include a phone tree, group text messages, or a designated online platform. Make sure all members of the network have access to the necessary contact information and understand their role in the communication process.

Sharing Emergency Plans and Procedures

Ensure that all members of your support network are familiar with your child's school emergency plans and procedures, as well as your family's personalized safety plan. This may include sharing copies of the school's emergency response guide, discussing lockdown and evacuation procedures, and providing contact information for school officials.

Practicing and Updating Your Support Network Plan

Periodically review and update your support network plan to ensure that it remains effective and relevant. This may involve adding or removing members, updating contact information, or modifying roles and responsibilities. Practice your plan with your support network, both individually and as a group, to ensure that everyone is prepared to act quickly and efficiently during an emergency.

Conclusion

Building a support network for emergencies is a crucial aspect of ensuring your child's safety during school emergencies. By identifying key members, assigning roles and responsibilities, creating a communication plan, and sharing emergency plans and procedures, you can help create a strong foundation of support that will benefit your child during times of crisis. In the next chapter, we will explore how to help children cope with the emotional aftermath of a school shooting or other traumatic events, as well as resources for mental health support and counseling services.

Chapter 4: Coping with the Emotional Aftermath of Traumatic Events

Introduction

School shootings and other traumatic events can have a profound and lasting impact on children's emotional well-being. As parents, it is essential to understand how to help your child process and cope with the aftermath of such events. This chapter will provide guidance on how to provide emotional support, facilitate conversations, and recognize signs of trauma and stress in children.

Providing Emotional Support

It's essential to provide emotional support to your child during and after a traumatic event. Listen to your child's concerns and validate their feelings. Reassure them that you are there to help and that you will do everything you can to keep them safe. It's also important to take care of your own emotional needs, so you can be a stable and reliable source of support for your child.

Facilitating Conversations

Encourage your child to talk about the traumatic event, but don't force them to discuss it if they're not ready. Create a safe and supportive environment for these conversations by actively listening and showing empathy. Explain the event in a way that is age-appropriate and accurate, without sharing unnecessary details that may be distressing.

Recognizing Signs of Trauma and Stress

Traumatic events can have a significant impact on children's emotional and physical well-being. Be aware of the signs of trauma and stress in your child, such as difficulty sleeping, increased anxiety or fear, changes in behavior or mood, or physical symptoms like headaches or stomachaches. If you notice any of these signs, seek professional help from a counselor or therapist trained in trauma-informed care.

Promoting Self-Care

Encourage your child to engage in self-care activities that promote emotional well-being, such as exercise, relaxation techniques, and creative outlets like art or music. Model healthy coping strategies for your child by taking care of your own mental and physical health.

Accessing Resources for Support

There are many resources available to support children and families coping with traumatic events. Reach out to your child's school counselor or mental health professional for additional support and guidance. Consider joining a support group for parents or connecting with other families who have experienced similar events.

Conclusion

Helping children cope with the emotional aftermath of traumatic events is a critical aspect of preparing for emergencies. By providing emotional support, facilitating conversations, recognizing signs of trauma and stress, promoting self-care, and accessing resources for support, parents can help their children navigate the challenging emotional landscape of trauma. In the next chapter, we will explore resources for mental health support and counseling services.

Chapter 5: Mental Health Support and Counseling Services

Introduction

Traumatic events can have a lasting impact on children's mental health, and it's essential to have access to resources and support when needed. In this chapter, we will explore mental health support and counseling services available to children and families who have experienced trauma.

Seeking Professional Help

If your child is struggling with the emotional aftermath of a traumatic event, it may be helpful to seek professional help from a mental health professional. Look for a therapist or counselor who specializes in trauma-informed care and has experience working with children. Your child's school counselor or pediatrician may be able to provide referrals.

Finding Support Groups

Support groups can be a valuable resource for children and families coping with trauma. Look for local support groups that specialize in trauma-informed care or connect with online support groups. These groups can provide a safe and supportive space to share experiences and connect with others who have had similar experiences.

Accessing Crisis Hotlines

Crisis hotlines can provide immediate support and guidance during times of emotional distress. Save crisis hotline numbers in your phone or post them in a prominent location in your home. The National Suicide Prevention Lifeline (1-800-273-8255) and the Crisis Text Line (text HOME to 741741) are both available 24/7.

Online Resources

There are many online resources available to support children and families coping with trauma. The National Child Traumatic Stress Network provides resources and information on trauma-informed care, and the American Psychological Association has resources on coping with trauma and stress. It's important to use caution when seeking information online and to verify the credibility of any sources.

Insurance Coverage

Check with your insurance provider to see what mental health services are covered under your plan. Some plans may cover therapy or counseling sessions, and some employers offer employee assistance programs that provide access to mental health resources.

Conclusion

Accessing mental health support and counseling services is a critical aspect of preparing for emergencies and coping with the emotional aftermath of traumatic events. Seek professional help when needed, find support groups, save crisis hotline numbers, use online resources with caution, and check your insurance coverage for mental health services. By utilizing these resources, parents can support their children's mental health and well-being during challenging times.

Chapter 6: Strengthening Family Resilience in the Face of Adversity

Introduction

In today's world, families must be prepared to face various challenges and adversities, including the unfortunate reality of school safety and gun violence. One key factor in navigating these challenges is resilience, which can be thought of as the ability to bounce back and recover from stress, adversity, or trauma. Resilience is a vital trait for both parents and children and plays a crucial role in maintaining a family's emotional well-being.

This chapter will provide you with practical strategies to strengthen your family's resilience in the face of adversity. By focusing on your own emotional well-being, modeling resilience for your children, and creating a supportive family environment, you can help your family heal and grow together.

Focus on Your Own Emotional Well-Being

As a parent, it's essential to prioritize your own emotional well-being to effectively support your children. Consider these strategies to maintain a strong emotional foundation:

Practice self-care: Engage in activities that help you relax and recharge, such as exercise, meditation, or hobbies you enjoy.
Seek support: Connect with friends, family, or support groups to share your feelings and experiences.
Manage stress: Identify your stressors and develop healthy coping mechanisms, such as deep breathing exercises or journaling.

Model Resilience for Your Children

Children learn from observing their parents' behavior. By demonstrating resilience, you can teach your children valuable life skills. Here are some ways to model resilience:

Display a positive attitude: Focus on the positives and express gratitude, even in challenging situations.
Embrace change: Adapt to changes and view them as opportunities for growth.
Develop problem-solving skills: Show your children how to approach challenges by brainstorming solutions and taking action.

Create a Supportive Family Environment

A strong family unit can provide a safe haven for each member, fostering resilience and growth. Here are some tips for creating a supportive family environment:

Encourage open communication: Foster an environment where family members feel comfortable sharing their feelings, thoughts, and concerns.
Be empathetic: Listen to your children and validate their emotions, helping them feel understood and supported.
Build strong connections: Spend quality time together and engage in family activities that promote bonding.
Establish routines: Routines provide a sense of stability and security, which can be especially important during times of adversity.

Teach Your Children Coping Strategies

Help your children develop healthy coping mechanisms to manage stress and adversity:

Encourage expression: Encourage your children to express their feelings through talking, writing, or drawing.
Teach relaxation techniques: Introduce your children to age-appropriate relaxation techniques, such as deep breathing or mindfulness exercises.
Promote problem-solving skills: Help your children analyze problems, brainstorm solutions, and make informed decisions.

Seek Professional Help if Needed

If your family is struggling to cope with adversity, consider seeking professional help. A mental health professional can provide valuable support, guidance, and resources for building resilience and addressing emotional challenges.

Conclusion

By focusing on your own emotional well-being, modeling resilience for your children, and creating a supportive family environment, you can help your family navigate adversity with strength and grace. Remember that resilience is not an innate trait but rather a skill that can be developed and nurtured over time. Be patient with yourself and your family as you work together to build and maintain resilience in the face of life's challenges.